Mommy Tell Me

A Story of Love and Learning

Written by: Nadine Vaughan Williams

Illustrated by: Heather Vaughan Manrique

AuthorHouse™ LLC
1663 Liberty Drive
Bloomington, IN 47403
www.authorhouse.com
Phone: 1-800-839-8640

Published by AuthorHouse 04/10/2014

ISBN: 978-1-4969-0429-4 (sc)
ISBN: 978-1-4969-0430-0 (e)

authorHOUSE®

Dedicated to
Velna Pearl Jones Williams Reniak
1919 – present

In honor of her 95 Years on Earth!

PART ONE

Mommy, tell me . . .

Of all the questions children ask their mommies, there is one hardly ever asked: "Mommy, would you tell me about your life?" That is because Moms work so hard to bring up their children as best they can, that they have little time for telling stories about themselves. They are much more interested in knowing what is happening in your life: Important things like: "Are you safe?" "Are you well?" Yes, even "Did you do your homework?" They want to know these things because your answers to their questions may tell them how they can help you better. Sometimes, knowing the answers might even help them protect you from harm. However, because Mommy does not talk much about her own life you may learn not to ask her about it either.

Sure, once in awhile she might say something like "When I was little, I had to do this or that", but it's usually just a way to let you know about something you are doing. I imagine she tells you very little about what really matters in her life; other than of course, that you matter . . . very much! Did you know that your Mom may be the most interesting and exciting person you will ever know? She may be filled with secrets, adventures, and lots of fun stuff. You think not? How much do you really know about her?

I will tell you a secret: I am a Mommy and I did not tell my son, a top notch pilot who flies very fast airplanes, that I too learned to fly airplanes when I was young. When he was a teen and told me about his plans to take flying lessons, I listened happily and encouraged him to feel proud of what he was doing. Yet, even though there were things I might have been able to teach him, it never occurred to me that he would be interested in knowing those things from me. Much later, when he did find out, he was plenty surprised!

Speaking of teaching, did you know that you and your Mom teach each other? When you were born, before the end of your first day of your life, you already knew her scent (that is a nice way of saying how she smells), and you could pick her out from all the other new Mommies! When you were hungry, you simply followed her scent to know where to go for food. Do you know why? It is because, one way or another, Mommies will always find a way to feed their babies. You actually taught your Mommy what you needed even though you did not say a word. You let her know by the kinds of sounds you made and by the expressions you put on your face. Expressions are things like smiles or frowns or the way you pucker up for a kiss.

Yes, when you were a baby, it was your sounds and your expressions that taught Mommy when you were hungry, wet, or even sleepy. You also taught her whether you were mad, sad, or glad. What do you think is the expression Mommies love to see the most? For me, it is a smile. That tells me when my child is happy. It also lets me know I am doing something right. Have you asked your Mommy which one of your expressions she likes the best?

Of course, not all Mommies teach their children in the same way. That is because Mommies teach life lessons the way life was taught to them. Some yell a lot whether they are mad and even when they are happy, while others may never yell at all. Like I said, they usually teach you the way their Mommies taught them when they were growing up. Sometimes we may not like the way our Mommies teach us, however, it is important to always remember one thing: They are doing the best they can. Just as you do the best you can to be the best person you can be, so does your Mommy. Sometimes you know you make a mistake, like when you throw a ball inside and knock something over or when you draw a picture and the colored lines get on the table or the wall.

Did you know that like you, your Mommy (or Daddy) might make a mistake too? If you are lucky, Mommy will tell you when she does, so you will not feel confused. But some Mommies are afraid to say when they make a mistake. That is because they believe that parents should always be right. They probably believe that their own parents were always right. Do you think anybody is always right? Probably not.

So, while your Mom does her best with you, she may make a mistake too. After all, there is no special training that a girl must go through before she can become a mother. When her children come into her life, she may not be much more than a child, herself. That is one of the reasons why being a Mom is the hardest job in the world. Think about it. Some people complain because they have to work too many hours at the office or are expected to know things that they were never taught. If they have no children, at least these people know they can go home after a long day and relax. It is different if the person is a Mom. That is because Moms' hours are longer than any other job on the planet and the decisions Moms must make are often difficult and with no warning. Even when a Mommy is able to spend as much time as she wants with her children, not all Mommies get a break . . . even to go to the bathroom! That may sound funny but it's true!

Then there are the Mommies who must work away from home: That is like having a job that lasts 24 hours a day, every day. While you are thinking, think about this: When you get sick or miss the school bus, who is the person most likely to get the call to come pick you up? That's right, it's your Mommy! The most amazing thing of all is that Mommies love you so much that they would not give you up for all the money in the world.

Yes, your Mommy knows she has to try to get it right the first time and sometimes that may make her feel scared or sad or even mad, especially if she feels worn out. Yet, she happily welcomes you into her world and smiles every time she tells anybody about the first time she saw you, for the rest of her life! Why? Because she believes that your life is worth it . . . all of the work, heartache, long hours, and pain! Did you know that if she could, your Mom would gladly jump in a river to save you; she would struggle with every ounce of her strength to get you away from a dangerous dragon; and she would instantly go to battle with anybody or anything that dared to attack you. You might think, "Sure, but that's because she gave birth to me. I came from her so I am a part of her."

While that is true for most children, did you know that sometimes a child's Mommy is not the person who gave birth to him? Although no one wants it to happen, once in awhile the woman who gives birth is simply not able to care for her baby. For some reason, that woman does not have all that she needs to bring her baby up in a way that gives her or him what she needs to grow up healthy, strong, and secure. When that happens, the birth mother must make a difficult decision — maybe the hardest one of her life. Once she decides, she does everything she can to find the right Mommy for her baby.

Sometimes the right Mommy is a Grandmother who has lots more love to give. Sometimes she is somebody's aunt because she is more the same age as the birth mother. Sometimes the best Mommy possible is even a big sister or a woman without children, who wants a child more than anything. Whoever that chosen woman is, that is who the child will learn to call Mommy and that special Mommy becomes the person who does all of the important things you have just been reading about. Are you getting the idea? There is no one more special than the person who loves you so much that she will care for you, feed you, clothe you and listen to you whether you are happy, scared, excited, or sad . . . no matter what else is going on in her life. So, not just on Mother's Day, but everyday of the year, let's hear it for Mommies everywhere. Hip! hip! Hooray!!!

Yet, for all the long hours, the danger and the sacrifice, Mommies do not receive silver stars or special awards for their efforts; and they get no pay at all! So why do Moms do all of this? It is because in their heart of hearts, what Mommies want more than anything, is for their little ones to have the best lives possible. That means that sometimes the only reward your Mommy gets is to see what a good person you are becoming; a person who cares about others as much as you care about yourself. So what better way could there be for you to show Mommy that you care about others, than to care about her life. That is why it is important to listen when your Mommy speaks and why it is important to ask her about herself. See if you can find out who your Mommy is when she is not being Mommy; what she feels passionate about. Is it flying or sewing or singing? Who was she before you came into her life? And what does she see herself doing in her wildest day dreams?

When I asked myself these questions about my own Mom, I realized that I did not know the answers and it was about time I learned more; like how she feels about her life . . . really feels. What does she hope the future might hold; not just for herself but for her children and even for the world? Before I asked her, I thought back over the years, through times of happiness and sorrow in my own life; as I grew from a small child to a teen and beyond. I knew there were times when I wished my Mom would not act so strict or get as angry as she did. Yet, when I stopped and thought about it, I now knew she was doing the best she could, trying to guide me into adulthood in the best ways she knew how. That is why I finally decided to pop the question: "Mommy, would you tell me about your life?" You know what? She did. My Mom told me the most amazing stories I'd ever heard. I began to wish I had asked her much sooner. In the following pages, you will hear some of what she said.

PART TWO

Mommy, told me . . .

"My name is Velna Pearl Jones Williams Reniak and I was born almost a hundred years ago. Back then, there were no TVs, computers, cell phones or I-Pads. We went to bed when the sun went down and we woke up with the crow of the rooster, when it was still dark. As the sun crept up over the barn and shined into my room, my hair would begin to sparkle like a glorious reflection. My eyes were the color of a clear summer day, my skin was tan and as smooth as silk, and years later, when I got old enough to date, the boys would tell me that I was the prettiest girl around. I guess I had to take their word for it since we didn't have many mirrors in the house. In my day, people said you were vain if you looked at yourself when you didn't have to.

I was blessed to grow up on a farm in a place called Florida. It was there, that centuries before, some of my ancestors sailed into a seaport just down the road. They landed on a small island and for the first time, they finally felt like they were home. Because they were horse breeders, when they stepped foot on dry land for the first time in many months, they let their horses run free too. Those fillies were so happy that they took off as fast as lightening and ran as far as they could see. Some ran so far that they were never found again and even to this day, their offspring still run wild on that little island.

Back then, my great, great, great grandfather was trying to escape from a land where the lives of good people were in danger from an angry king. You can't even imagine the terrible way they had to live back then in what they called the old country. There were so many people who did have enough to eat that they left their homes and set off across the sea in ships, rather than be thrown into harsh prisons for trying to feed their families. That is why when they arrived here, they thought it was the most beautiful place they had ever seen. It is beautiful still.

It was wild too. Even in the year 1919 — that's when I was born — it was teeming with five kinds of poisonous snakes, Florida panthers, raccoons, possums, and a bunch of alligators. That's because the place where our little farm was built sat next to a deep, dark swamp. Yep. that's the place I grew up calling home. I am glad that all those years before, my ancestors had decided to live inland, rather than on the island because Florida has something called hurricanes. Those are crazy, strong winds that can blow away your house if it's in the way. Back then, our family was not the only one who lived in those woods, either. There were other people who lived there way before we built our little homestead.

In the surrounding woods lived the real natives of this land. Some people called them Indians. Their Native name was Timucua. Like all people, most of them were patient with our strange ways and even liked to trade stuff with us. There were a few who turned out to be not so nice but I know they had good reasons for it. Terrible things were done to many of their people by those who thought only of themselves. It makes me sad when I think about it now.

But back to my life. In the early 1900s, when I was still a child, I thought it was a paradise too, even though it was filled with danger and lots of hard work. I was lucky because the first thing I saw each morning was the face of my Momma. By the time I got into the kitchen, she had already collected eggs from the hen house, churned butter for breakfast, and put grits on the old cook stove. From the times when I was sick, I learned that even before the sun was up, Momma and Daddy would go into the kitchen together. They said it was to get the fire started but I knew it was their special time together.

Every morning, as the coffee came to a boil and the wood stove heated up the room, my Momma would shave my Daddy's weathered face with a straight razor while he sat there reading the Good Book to her. That started when my Momma was a sixteen year old bride and went on until she had a stroke in her late 80s. This was something they did every day and they never grew tired of it. Their love was something special too. Even after her stroke, any time my Daddy went anywhere near my Momma's chair, he would pat down his hair and try to look his best for his still beautiful bride of more than 75 years.

I think it led to my staying married for such a very long time too. Until the day my husband died, I cared for him, prepared his food, and fed him when he could no longer hold a spoon. He was a good man too. He was different from my Daddy in many ways, but he was a good man. Like my Daddy, he worked hard, loved me more than life, and he never wavered in his spiritual devotion. Maybe that's what keeps a couple together regardless of what else may try to tear them apart: Hard work; unconditional love; and believing deeply that there is more to life than what we can see.

Back then, families grew big so that there was always help on the farm. So after breakfast, even though the sun was not fully up, some of my sisters and brothers went outside to help Daddy milk the cows; some of us helped Momma in the kitchen; while the rest of us helped sweep out the sand that always found its way back inside. Finally, after everything was done, we washed up and dressed in our good clothes so we could go to school. Of course, we walked, even though our school was miles away. It was kind of exciting since in the early morning mist, we sometimes saw a black Florida panther staring at us from just beyond the barn.

During the summers, we did not go to school so our chores also included planting vegetables and repairing equipment or corralling the cows and bringing them home. As for me? What I loved most was spending time with my Daddy. Whether I helped him plant in the fields, work with the horses, or repair the fences, I felt like Daddy's special girl. I loved him so much that I would even try to go to work with him! He knew it was because I loved him so he would always smile and say, "Sorry, Sunshine, but you are just too little." Now, something you should know about me is that if anybody ever told me that I could not do something, I would find a way to do it. That is because if you believe you can do it, all things are possible.

One day when my Daddy wasn't looking, I hid in his car when he was getting ready to go to work. Besides being a farmer, he had a second job with the US Postal Service as a Rural Mail Carrier. That day, the cows had gotten out and Daddy had to round them up, so he was in a hurry. In his haste, he didn't check to see where I was and it wasn't until he was all the way to work that he discovered me on the floor board, in the back of his car. I had been lying on the floor in back of his seat as Daddy travelled over rickety old rails, through the swamps, over highways, and on bumpy dirt roads. At first, I thought he was going to be mad and he did act like it a little, mostly because he was afraid that his little girl could have fallen out and gotten lost or worse. Secretly, I think he was happy that all I wanted in the world was just to be with him so much that I even tried to go to his work. I guess I proved that even though I was only 5 years old, I was already very independent!

I remember another fun thing we did when I was a bit bigger. All of us kids; sisters, brothers, and cousins, would pile onto Daddy's big flatbed truck and drive over even more rickety old roads all the way to Fernandina Beach. There, we would walk out on the jetties and fish with long cane poles. Except for church, my Momma didn't go with us to most places, but she sure did like to fish! That was funny and fun. Most of the time, she was way too busy in the kitchen or gathering eggs from the hen house outside, or milking the cow, churning butter or cooking the best tasting meals you could imagine. One thing about my Momma; she was a strong woman in her body, mind, and spirit and nobody ever questioned her judgement or talked back to her. Eventually, we all learned that lesson.

As I mentioned, because back then there was no school bus to take kids to school, we had to walk whether it rained or froze. Each day, every one of us walked through that magical forest that was filled with mystery, over that dark and dangerous swamp. As we passed through, the alligators would swim lazily around the swamp while the snakes looped themselves around nearby tree limbs. I remember hearing the stories before I was old enough to go to school. So even then, I knew I had to learn to be brave so I could do it too when I was old enough to go to school.

Finally the big day came: My first day of school. Surrounded by my brothers and sisters, I walked down that long country road to the old swamp. There, they taught me how to spot the biggest logs to step on as we made our way to the other side. I had to jump from one log to the next, even while carrying school books, since my legs were still too short to step across. At first, it was spooky since the alligators and snakes lurked only feet away. It may even sound scary to you. But once I started doing it, I didn't think of myself as being brave; it's just the way things were. I probably would have felt more scared if I had to cross a big city street!

On one particular day, after a big storm had scattered the logs willy nilly across the old swamp; the most amazing thing happened. When my sister Wynell, stepped on a log, it started to move with her on it! That log turned out to be a big old alligator who did not like being stepped on! That's the day I discovered that whether or not I was brave, I was certainly fast! You would have thought I was the one to step on that old gator. I ran across the rest of the logs and onto dry land so fast that the other kids barely saw me. To this day, every time somebody mentions it, I want to laugh!

Back on the farm, after we got home from school, there was always work to do and we had to complete our chores before we could do anything else. The really nice thing about it is that we all worked together; Momma, Daddy, my sisters, my brothers, and me. Those were the days before most Moms and Dads had to go somewhere else to work; when little boys could see, first hand, what it meant to be a man, and we girls could see what it was like to be a woman. There were times during the school year when we didn't even have to go to school because we were needed to help out on the farm. Everybody in the family who was big enough to walk was called on during those times. Whether it was with gathering all that my father had planted back in the Spring or with canning the fruit and vegetables we had just harvested; we knew that it took everybody in the family, working toward the same goal, to keep our family fed and clothed. It's too bad more children don't get to share that feeling since it is the best way for a child to know "I really matter."

As I grew into a young woman, my body became strong like my Momma. As the captain of my school's basketball team, we showed all the other schools in the County just what the girls from Callahan were made of. Our team won almost every game for a spell. After I got married, moved away, and had a few children, I got to use those skills as a playground director for the City of Tampa; for over twenty years! Even now, it seems like everywhere I go, people say 'Hello Mrs. Williams' 'Good Morning, Mrs Williams'." But wait, I'm getting ahead of myself. First, I went from being Farmer Jones daughter to Mr. Williams' wife.

The day I met the man of my dreams I was down in Tampa with my older sister, visiting our Aunt Isabelle. She asked me to walk to the store for some things so I did. That's where I saw him! He was the most amazing man I'd ever met. There he stood: Tall and fit, with coal black hair, a ruddy complexion, and deep, dark brown eyes. When I looked him in those eyes and he looked right back, I thought I would swoon. Soon, every time he looked at me, I noticed that he had a dreamy kind of smile. That's when I knew that he felt it too. It's what some people call love at first sight. Although he was a young man in his twenties, he already owned his own store and even had his own house.

You can imagine my disappointment when I learned that he was set to have a blind date with my sister that very night! Neither of us knew what to do. But you know what? Somehow it all worked out because we ended up getting married and had six children together! We felt like Romeo and Juliet, except with a happier ending. Yes, within a year of meeting me, he had 'scooped up that pretty little girl from Callahan' (me) and asked her to be his wife. Of course, I said 'Yes' and we started our married life in the city where he lived. I didn't know it then, but I was in for a shock.

As a farmer's daughter, straight from the farm, I had known a completely different life; a life where we worked together as a family and dating was chaperoned. That means an adult always went along anytime a girl went out with a boy. On the other hand, Romeo, I mean my husband, had been a bachelor for many years and was used to doing what he wanted when he wanted to do it. Suddenly, I went from carefree to care giver. Within a few short years, I had a home to care for by myself, a husband and six children, most born within a few years after marrying. I became more tired than I had ever been helping around the farm. When hard times fell on the store, and I had to take on an outside job too, I became a reluctant role model for all working moms to follow.

Funny thing is when I look back over my life, those were some of the best times I had. I couldn't have found a job I loved more. Teaching a room full of four and five year old children may not have been for everyone, but I loved it. I knew I was helping prepare them for elementary school and in the afternoons, on the playground, I got to show the bigger kids the right way to throw a ball. I loved every last one of those children, big and small.

I must admit, I felt proud when I heard my daughter say one time: 'My Mom is beautiful, smart, brave, athletic and at times she must have felt a little bit crazy with so many new responsibilities.' I guess she was right; I certainly did feel overwhelmed at times, especially as my six daughters became teenagers. The hours I worked got crazier too. And although there were times when I felt as if I could not do one more thing, I held onto my belief that if we keep our eye on the prize and keep on working, we will make it through . . . ."

. . . and that's where my Mom's story ends, at least, for now.

PART THREE

Mom, have I told you . . . ?

"Dearest Mom . . . have I told you what it was like for me to have such a super Mom? If I haven't it is because I didn't fully realize it until after I got married and started having children of my own. That is when I began to understand just how amazing you have always been. And as I continue to learn about my own weaknesses, my strengths and how courageous I must be when hard times hit, I feel closer to you. I finally understand the extent of the sacrifices you made to keep us safe . . . ."

Over the years, as I began to talk with my Mom more as a person for whom I have great respect, and less as a daughter to her mother, my memories began to change. I found that once painful memories began to fade away. They were replaced by new understanding and unconditional love. Because we did not always agree, our talks became even more lively and meaningful. This happened even when I moved over 3000 miles away. In 1974, in pursuit of my own life goals, I ended up living away from my mom and my family for almost 30 years. Yet my mom's presence was with me there even more strongly than when she and I had been in the same room together, before we learned to really talk with each other.

I looked forward to the times she would come stay with me. At those times, uninterrupted by the customs of the old south, we would talk about anything under the sun. I was amazed when she seemed to like it too! I even took her to a life drawing class with me and saw her courage when she walked in like she'd been doing it her whole life. I saw a wit about her that she often kept hidden when she was being everybody's mom. It's funny, because as I returned to school and earned one degree after another, seeking out strong women to model after, that's when it hit me. I was jolted by the knowledge that I already had the best role model of all!

Of course, there were times that were hard for her to talk about; like when she and Dad did not know if they would have enough money to support our big family. Those times were not easy for anyone but I think they weighed on my Mom the most. Even though they tried not to talk about it in front of us kids, I knew she was struggling. As a farmer's daughter, she never thought she would wonder if we would have enough to eat. But when the big grocery chains came into our neighborhood and took my dad's customers away, he had to close his store even though many people in the neighborhood still owed him thousands of dollars. He allowed it because he had such a kind and generous heart but it was hard for my mom to witness the result of those choices.

Yet, even in the midst of it all, she found a way to send me to dance class because she knew that was the most important thing in my world. She did that because, through it all, her most important job in life was making sure that we had enough. And because my Daddy continued to work hard, they loved each other through those hard times. I learned much later how tiring this was for them both. As children, we were just glad that we had enough food on the table and that we had parents who loved us. It was during those times that Mom encouraged us to learn how to make our own clothes and budget our money. Those were both skills I have prized many times over the years. During those years, as Daddy struggled to make ends meet, Momma became the center of all of our lives around which everything else circled.

As she got older, my Mom told me even more stories, but I already knew what felt most important of all. She taught all five of my sisters and me how to be modern women without even knowing it; how to be hard-working, strong, independent, smart and loving even when the road was not smooth and the path was not easy. She taught us to have faith that life would work out if we kept living it to the best of our abilities.

From our mother, the best mom we could have asked for, we learned what it meant to be a woman in ways that few people ever get to experience. For that, I am forever grateful. So, Mom, on the occasion of your 95th Birthday, I want to thank you! I am so glad you are mine. Like a living Valentine, you will always be in my heart, no matter where we are, whether on this old earth or in another place. I am so glad I thought to finally ask you to tell me about your life.

How about you, Dear Reader? How much do you know about your mom?

Why not try asking her about it? This is how you do it:

"Mommy, would you tell me about your life?"

THE END

Printed in the United States
By Bookmasters